Animal Look-Alikes
Frogs and Toads

Joanne Mattern

RED
CHAIR
•PRESS•

Animal Look-Alikes is produced and published by Red Chair Press:

Red Chair Press LLC   PO Box 333   South Egremont, MA 01258-0333

www.redchairpress.com

About the Author

Joanne Mattern is the author of nearly 350 books for children and teens. She began writing when she was a little girl and just never stopped! Joanne loves nonfiction because she enjoys bringing science topics to life and showing young readers that nonfiction is full of compelling stories! Joanne lives in the Hudson Valley of New York State with her husband, four children, and several pets, which look nothing alike!

Publisher's Cataloging-In-Publication Data
Names: Mattern, Joanne, 1963-
Title: Frogs and toads / Joanne Mattern.

Description: [South Egremont, Massachusetts] : Red Chair Press, [2018] | Series: Animal look-alikes | Interest age level: 006-010. | Includes science vocabulary, fun facts, and trivia about each type of animal. | "Core content library." | Includes bibliographical references. | Summary: "Webbed feet. Slimy or dry. Lives on land or in water. Is it a frog or a toad? Look inside to learn how these cold-blooded animals are alike and how they differ."--Provided by publisher.

Identifiers: LCCN 2016947289 | ISBN 978-1-63440-211-8 (library hardcover) | ISBN 978-1-63440-216-3 (ebook)

Subjects: LCSH: Frogs--Juvenile literature. | Toads--Juvenile literature. | CYAC: Frogs. | Toads.

Classification: LCC QL668.E2 M38 2018 (print) | LCC QL668.E2 (ebook) | DDC 597.8--dc23

Illustrations by Tim Haggerty.

Map illustration by Joe LeMonnier.

Photo credits: Shutterstock except for the following: p. 5, 14, 15, 16: Ingimage; p. 13: Minden Pictures.

Printed in Canada

102017 1P FRNS18

Table of Contents

Frog or Toad?

Can you tell these two animals apart? One of these animals is a frog. The other animal is a toad. Frogs and toads have a lot in common. But they are not the same! Frogs and toads may look and act alike, but there are many things about them that are different. Let's learn all about these unusual animals and what makes each one special!

Amazing Amphibians

Frogs and toads are both **amphibians**. Amphibians have some interesting features. One important fact about amphibians is that they are cold-blooded. This means that they cannot control their body temperature. If an amphibian sits in the hot sun, its body temperature goes up. If it is in a cold place, its body temperature goes down. To keep their body at the right temperature, amphibians often have to move in and out of the sun or find a cool place in the water or on the ground to cool off.

Common toad

European green tree frog

The most amazing thing about amphibians is their life cycle. These animals go through some big changes as they grow up! A baby frog or toad does not look anything like an adult. Baby frogs and toads are called tadpoles. Tadpoles have no legs, but they do have a tail. Tadpoles also have no lungs. Instead, they have gills and breathe water just like a fish. Tadpoles live underwater.

As time passes, the tadpole's body changes. Its tail disappears. It grows four legs. It develops lungs and starts breathing air. When the tadpole is an adult frog or toad, it can live on land. It takes some species of tadpoles just a few weeks to grow into frogs and toads. Other tadpole species take up to eight months.

Power Word: The word "amphibian" means "two lives." Why is this a good name?

The Life Cycle of a Frog

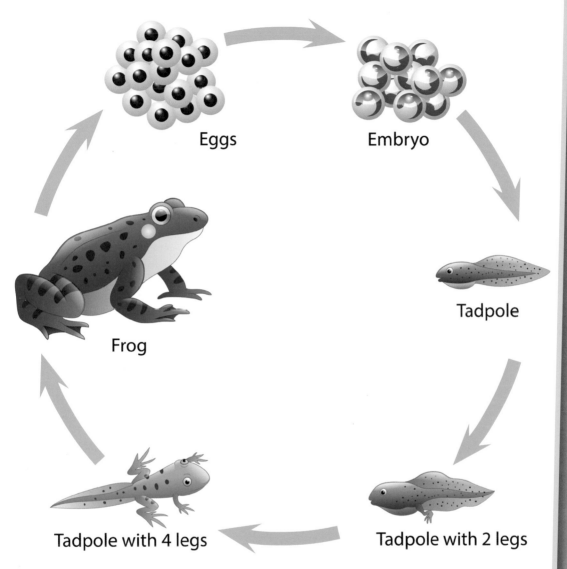

Eggs

Embryo

Tadpole

Frog

Tadpole with 4 legs

Tadpole with 2 legs

Now You Know!

Long ago, amphibians were the first animals with backbones to leave the sea and live on land.

Cape river frog

Common brown toad

NOW YOU KNOW!

Some tree frogs can jump over 7 feet (2 m).
That's almost 50 times the length of their bodies!

Different Bodies

One way to tell an adult frog from a toad is to look at its body. Most frogs have a long, thin body. A frog's back legs are much longer than its front legs. Those long legs help the frog be a great jumper. Frogs are good swimmers too. They often have webbed feet that help them swim.

A toad's body is very different. A toad's body is wide and round. Its legs are much shorter than a frog's. That means that toads can hop and walk, but they cannot jump. Most toads also do not have webbed feet. They don't need them because they do not spend much time swimming.

Frogs and toads also have different eyes. A frog's eyes are higher and rounder than a toad's, and they often bulge out.

Frogs and toads come in many different sizes. In 2012, scientists discovered the world's smallest frog in Papua New Guinea. This frog is about the same size as a fly. The largest frog is the African Goliath frog. This huge frog can grow to three feet (1 m) long and weigh up to seven pounds (3.2 kg)!

The largest toads live in Central and South America. They can grow up to 11 inches (28 cm) long. The smallest toad is less than an inch (2.5 cm) long.

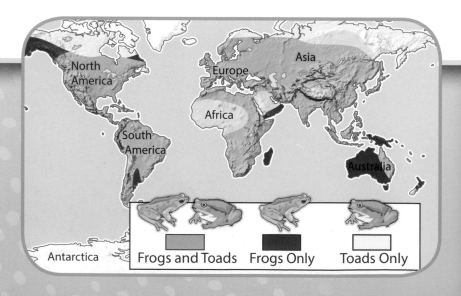

North America

Europe

Asia

Africa

South America

Australia

Antarctica

Frogs and Toads   Frogs Only   Toads Only

African Goliath frog

Smooth or Rough?

Touching one of these animals is another way to tell if it is a frog or a toad. A frog has smooth, wet skin. Some frogs look slimy because they are covered with a layer of **mucus**. This mucus keeps the frog's skin from drying out. A toad's skin is rough and dry. It is often covered with bumps.

Many frogs are brightly colored. Poison dart frogs live in the rain forest. Their skin can be bright blue, red, yellow, purple, or orange. Other frogs are bright green. Some toads are brightly colored, but most are not. A toad is likely to be brown or dark green.

Now You Know!

A poison dart frog's bright colors warn predators that its skin is covered with poisonous mucus. A toad's dull colors help it hide in the woods or the water.

Frogs have
smooth
skin.

Toads have bumpy,
rough skin.

Red striped
poison dart frog

Frogs live
near water.

Giant bufo toad

Home, Sweet Home

Frogs and toads are found almost everywhere in the world. They live on every continent except Antarctica. However, these amphibians do live in different places. Frogs have to live near water. They need the water to keep their skin from drying out. That is why you often see frogs in ponds or lakes. Many kinds of frogs live in the rain forest, where it is wet and warm all the time.

Toads do not need to stay wet. You are more likely to find a toad on land than in the water. Many kinds of toads live in the woods. These animals can even live in the desert! The Sonoran desert toad lives in the southwestern part of the United States, where it is very dry.

What's For Dinner?

Both frogs and toads are **carnivores**. That means they eat meat. Frogs and toads eat insects and spiders. They have a very interesting way of catching their **prey**!

Frogs and toads have long, sticky tongues. These amphibians sit very still, waiting for an insect to fly or crawl past. Frogs and toads have big eyes that help them see their prey. When the frog or toad sees its prey, it shoots its tongue out of its mouth and grabs the insect. Then it pulls its tongue back in and swallows its prey whole. A frog or toad can do this because its tongue is attached to the front of its jaw. This lets the frog or toad flip its tongue out very quickly.

The bigger the frog, the bigger its prey. Some large frogs can even eat baby turtles, mice, and smaller frogs.

Now You Know!

A frog closes its eyes when it swallows so its eye muscles can help push the food down its throat.

Red eyed tree frog
about to eat a cricket

African bull frog.

Staying Safe

Many **predators** like to eat frogs and toads. These predators live on both land and water. Many birds, such as herons, swans, and wading birds like to grab frogs out of the water. So do raccoons, snakes, opossums, and even larger frogs. When frogs are in the water, they also face danger from fish and turtles.

Snowy egret

Toads have many predators too. Large birds such as hawks and owls swoop down and grab toads to eat. Skunks, raccoons, and snakes also like to eat toads.

NOW YOU KNOW!

Some toads puff up their bodies to look bigger and scare predators away.

This small backyard toad is camouflaged against dried sticks and leaves.

To protect themselves, many frogs and toads have poison on their skin. This poison not only makes predators sick, it also makes the frog or toad taste very bad. Many frogs and toads also use **camouflage** to hide from predators.

Dyeing dart frog

**Toad who has woken
up from hibernation in
duckweed leaves**

Too Cold or Too Hot

Amphibians are cold-blooded, so they cannot control their body temperature. Frogs and toads cannot stay out during cold weather or they will freeze. To stay warm, frogs and toads **hibernate**. They find a safe place and go into a deep sleep. Their breathing slows down. Their hearts beat slower too. They do not eat or 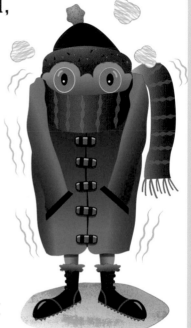 drink. When the weather gets warm, the frog or toad wakes up and hops away.

Frogs and toads also need to stay cool during hot weather. Amphibians that live in the desert often sleep during the hot, dry months. This state is called **estivation**. When rain falls and the temperature goes down, the frog or toad wakes up.

Finding a Mate

Frogs and toads breed in the spring. During this time, they look for a mate. In most species, the male frog puffs air into a sac of loose skin under his throat. The air moves across his vocal cords and makes a loud croaking sound. This special mating call lets females know the males are there and ready to mate. Other species of frogs use a different trick to find a mate. The males hop around and wave their legs in the air to get the females to notice them.

Painted reed frog

European common
frog waving legs to
attract mate

Male marsh frog
singing to female

Red eyed tree frog protects eggs on a leaf

Agile frog among newly laid eggs

Eggs and Tadpoles

Frogs and toads mate in the water. As they mate, the female lays a string of eggs in the water for the male to **fertilize**. Frog eggs and toad eggs look different. A frog lays its eggs in a big bunch. Toads lay their eggs in long chains.

Most frogs and toads lay their eggs and leave. They do not take care of the eggs or the tadpoles after they hatch. Many eggs and tadpoles are eaten by insects, fish, ducks, and other predators. However, some frogs and toads really do take care of their eggs. Some tree frogs carry their eggs on their backs until they hatch. Then they release the tadpoles into a stream or pond. Other frogs wrap their eggs around them or even carry them in a pouch under their throat.

Saving Frogs and Toads

Frogs and toads are important parts of our world. They help people by eating many insects. In turn, frogs and toads provide food for many different animals, including birds, reptiles, raccoons, and more.

Scientists are worried that frogs and toads are in danger. Over the years, many species have disappeared. Frogs and toads are **endangered** because they have no place to live. When people drain swamps or cut down forests, they take away animal homes.

Clearing a forest

Pollution is also a big problem. Frogs have thin skin that absorbs poisons caused by pollution. Because frogs and toads live in both water and on land, they are affected by pollution in both places. Scientists are working hard to save frogs and toads around the world. They want to make the world safe for both frogs and toads.

Special Animals

Frogs and toads may seem alike, but these animals are not the same. Many things about them are different, from their bodies to where they live. These amphibians are special parts of the natural world. Other animals and people depend on them in many ways. No matter what it looks like or how it behaves, each frog and toad has its own special place on our planet.

Green flying frog

Glossary

amphibians animals that spend the first part of their lives in the water and the second part on land

camouflage coloring or markings on an animal's skin that help it blend in with its surroundings

carnivores animals that eat other animals

endangered in danger of dying out

estivation a period of sleep when the weather is hot and dry

fertilize to join male and female cells together to produce young

hibernation a period of sleep when the weather is cold

mucus a slimy substance produced by the body

pollution harmful substances in the environment

predators animals that hunt other animals for food

prey animals that are hunted by other animals for food

Read More in the Library

Herrington, Lisa M. *Frogs and Toads: What's the Difference?* Children's Press, 2015.

Stewart, Melissa. *Frog or Toad?: How Do You Know?* Enslow, 2011.